IMAGES
of America

GREEKS IN QUEENS

IMAGES
of America

GREEKS IN QUEENS

Christina Rozeas
Foreword by Constantine E. Theodosiou

ARCADIA
PUBLISHING

Published by Arcadia Publishing
Charleston, South Carolina

Library of Congress Control Number: 2012938152

For all general information, please contact Arcadia Publishing:
Telephone 843-853-2070
Fax 843-853-0044
E-mail sales@arcadiapublishing.com
For customer service and orders:
Toll-Free 1-888-313-2665

Visit us on the Internet at www.arcadiapublishing.com

Home is where the heart is, so I lovingly dedicate this book to my amazing family, my brilliant husband, John, and especially my grandparents, who are watching over all of us from heaven.

CONTENTS

FOREWORD

I can still hear my grandmother's chuckle. She was raised in Arna, a mountaintop village roughly 25 miles south of Sparta. It came after my first asking her to relate what Far Rockaway was like in "her day" as she fondly referred to it. *Ma yiati, paidaki mou?* she asked. "What for, my little one?" (I was just 11.) "Focus instead on your future," she said. Unlike her laugh, this barely resonated in me. She didn't understand how her Americanized existence intrigued me; it still does. To be fair, I was at a loss to put this vague feeling into words in a way that she could understand. It was, however, what prompted me to save her photo albums after she died. Sure, some pictures lost their immediacy, yet somehow they still manage to convey the life she would come to know in this remote part of Queens. I am grateful to have them.

In time, I prevailed on *Yiayia* to satisfy my curiosity. Through her recollections, I caught a glimpse of mother and uncle as children, my grandfather in his shoe repair shop on Cornaga Avenue, Roche's Beach, firm friendships, and family feuds. I learned why Franklin Roosevelt was such an inspired leader. *Etan axios!* "He was worthy!" And how Yiayia became a naturalized citizen by answering, "You kidding? It's Eisenhower!" when asked the name of the president of the United States. As grateful as I was to hear these anecdotes, I've realized since then that she revealed no more than what she thought was necessary for me to hear. It was typical of many Greek immigrants of her generation, who saw wisdom in their discretion.

Much to the frustration of history seekers like me, Greeks have put little value in intellectualizing over their lot. Whether this was due to their sense of modesty, privacy, lack of spare time, or indifference, it explains why their role in the American storyline figures less prominently than, say, their Irish-, Jewish-, or Italian-American counterparts. Given that the Greeks too have maintained a presence here for over a century, it is astonishing to learn that this trend shifted only recently. That it has, we owe a debt of thanks to authors like Christina Rozeas and publishers like Arcadia. Done with a keen sense of purpose, their regional histories amply show that the Greek-American community goes beyond the sum total of Greek diners throughout the land. Finally!

The same holds true for this wonderful book. Suggestive of Jenny Marketou's revealing immigrant study published more than two decades ago, *The Great Longing: The Greeks of Astoria* (Kedros Publishing, 1987), Rozeas boldly took the next step and chronicled the lives of Greeks who strove to make their mark beyond Astoria's borders. This shouldn't be taken to mean that Astoria's days as our city's premier Greektown are numbered; far from it. This compilation is special in that it enhances the meaning of Greek New York—or what it means to be Greek in New York. And with it, Rozeas duly recognizes the longstanding Greek community with all its virtues and vitality.

—Constantine E. Theodosiou
President, Greater Astoria Historical Society

ACKNOWLEDGMENTS

This dream wouldn't have been possible without the endless support of my wonderful family. They've inspired me to always go above and beyond, and, just for that, I am truly thankful.

To the people who have listened to me prattle on and helped me in every way possible—I can't thank you enough! From my earliest mentors turned guardian angels: Christodoulos and Anna Themelis, and Mr. Paul Stratigeas, who set the foundations for my entire life. I will remember and cherish you always. To my present-day mentors, Patricia Volonakis-Davis and Jason Antos, for listening and inspiring—thank you. Caitrin Cunningham, my tireless editor, for everything she has taught me as well as her endless amount of patience. I have been honored to work with you.

Pulling a very busy community together for detailed information was no easy feat. By name, I would be more than honored to thank those who listened, contributed, and carried my sanity in their kindness: Constantine E. Theodosiou, Irene and William Tzivelekis, Stathoula and Chris Rozeas, Frank Ginis, William Ginis, Anna Feggaros, Lara Tewes, Father John Antonopoulos (for a huge miracle), Alison McKay of the Bayside Historical Society, Dora Themelis, Elias I. Katsos, Amy Wolf-Perschke, Sara Cedar Miller, Vivian Siempos, the Greek Cultural Center, Christina at the Queens College Center for Byzantine and Modern Greek Studies, G. Tzouganos, Calliope Makris, Emanuel Feggaros, and William Argyros.

I am the luckiest girl in the world when it comes to my handful of incredible friends, who have given me so much love that it's changed my life.

Speaking of love changing my life: to the most encouraging, supportive, and brilliant person in the world: my husband, John. His unending love, strength, and patience never cease to astound me. I love you more than words will or could ever say.

INTRODUCTION

Recently, it has come to pass that Greeks as a whole have been glamorized into two categories: the rough-and-tough survivors, and the passionate lovers. The truth is, Greece has birthed a nation not a stranger to war, slavery, and natural disasters, but also one with a rich history and culture, and a love and a passion for life. The Greeks have given the world drama, medicine, democracy, philosophy, math, and the Mediterranean diet.

During times of war and slavery, the love of our culture and religion never dwindled: there were hidden schools built in caves, in mountains, and underground in order to teach the future generations where we came from, with an emphasis on what we were fighting for; stories passed down from generations were constantly drilled into our minds, developing in us an undying hunger to learn all we could so that our future, our children, could be better. For many, the only solution to preserve our history and our country was to leave it. The Greeks did what they had to do to survive: they came to America.

With whispers that it was the "land of great opportunity" and only the clothes on their backs, floods of Greek immigrants came to America to build their future. Families and friends from the Old Country met others on their journey to this great land, and built "Little Greece" in Queens, New York.

Taking what they knew from their past, coupled with a strong work ethic, the Greek community of Queens slowly began to transform from laborers to business owners, striving to make enough money—money to provide their families with good homes, money to provide their children with a stellar education (with a major emphasis on the history of their culture), and enough left over to help out the remainder of their families in Greece. As their families grew, so did the need for more space—the Greeks of Astoria panned out to quickly cover the rest of Queens, always returning to their home base of Astoria to keep the community they worked hard to build alive and bustling.

And the rest, as they say, is history.

One

In the Beginning

A faded portrait from the early to mid-1920s sets the stage of the new family dynamic in Greece. Women were left behind during war, while their husbands and brothers were drafted as soldiers to protect and defend their country and their families the best way they knew how. This scenario inadvertently placed women in a leadership role in the home, teaching everything and anything they possibly could to their children in order to carry out the future. (Author's collection.)

In the mid-1950s, a group of women gather to bring in the new year with their families. For many Greeks, it was a treat to have a Christmas tree during the economic hardships that the war presented. It also may have been the last holiday season extended families spent together in their homeland. (Courtesy of Irene Tzivelekis.)

The Papadoulis children, pictured here, were one of the first families to pose for photographs in their native Leros, Dodecanese. Little did they know that their lives would not only bring them to a new country, but also that they would become standout members of the Astoria Greek Orthodox community, involved with as many events as they possibly could. Both siblings were steadfast in keeping their family strong and financially stable no matter the cost, even long after they migrated to New York. (Courtesy of Michael Papadoulis.)

The woman pictured here was likely the matriarch of a family. Photographed in the late 1920s in the Dodecanese islands of Greece, she led her family to safety financially, academically, and, physically, to a nearby cave when warlike activity deemed harmful was discovered via eavesdropping on neighboring soldiers. (Courtesy of Irene Tzivelekis.)

Greek men jumped at the chance to work on ships as a means of coming to America. Seen here are two Greek men who worked as chefs in exchange for meager wages and passage to the United States, in order to prepare for life in a new country for their families. (Courtesy of Michael Papadoulis.)

The young man in this image represents a person of good standing in Greece. Taken before World War I, this photograph predates the largest migration of Greek people to the United States during the time of the Great War in Europe. (Courtesy of Irene Tzivelekis.)

During the many years of wartime hardships that tore Greece apart, homes consisted not only of the immediate family. Oftentimes, extended family such as aunts and uncles, cousins, and especially grandparents would inhabit the homes. The family gathered in front of the home in this photograph is an example of those left behind in a time of war: women, children, and young men who weren't yet old enough to serve in the Greek army. (Courtesy of Anna Feggaros.)

Saving enough money to have a professional photograph taken during a time of war was an incredible luxury in the 1920s. This photograph of Irene Papadoulis and her daughter was probably arranged in order for their beloved husband and father to have something to look forward to while serving in the army. (Courtesy of Irene Tzivelekis.)

Though leaving their families behind in the only land they knew must have been the most difficult plight of a Greek man's life, an adventure to improve their own and their family's welfare was underway. In this photograph, while traveling to the Americas, Michael Papadoulis is seen with what was the first automobile he had the opportunity to ride in since being raised in a tiny Greek village. (Author's collection.)

14

On leave from the naval bases of Greece, many men, like those pictured here, would return home. In many cases, during wartime, the visit home would be the first time these courageous men would meet their own children before being shipped out, heartbreakingly leaving their entire lives behind to defend their country. (Author's collection.)

Thess men are gathered around a police station in Greece. Hearing news about the incredible opportunities that lay before them if they left for the United States awakened a hankering to gather their families and make their way toward a new life. (Author's collection.)

Greek men 18 years of age, like the one shown here, were expected to serve a mandatory two to three years in the army, training for any kind of circumstance. Conditions were harsh during the time of service, and many men counted down the days for it to be over. If men preferred to stay in the army, they gained rank and continued to serve professionally when their mandated years were over. (Courtesy of Anna Feggaros.)

Greek men who moved to America, in most cases to New York, and fell in love with their new country proudly served in the US army. The man in this c. 1950 photograph is pictured wearing his uniform, standing outside his New York residence. (Courtesy of Stathoula Rozeas.)

In the 1940s, many men who had migrated from Greece were drafted for World War II. Pictured here are a group of men on leave from their honorable duty as servicemen. (Courtesy of Irene Tzivelekis.)

The pain of losing a family member was a heartache that was all too familiar to Greek women. Pictured here is a widow, dressed entirely in black—which she knew she would likely be for the rest of her life, as is the Greek custom. (Courtesy of Irene Tzivelekis.)

Families were often photographed together, unless there were circumstances keeping them apart. Pictured is a composition of photographs of three siblings taken at different times and pieced together by the photographer. The man to the left seems to be wearing a uniform, which means that he left soon after for war. Judging by the suit of the man on the right, he was the older male of the family. As the breadwinner, the law stated that he was to stay behind and provide for the family. (Author's collection.)

Pictured above is the new dynamic of a family: women. While men were toiling to raise enough wages, working on their farms and at other jobs, women stayed home, teaching their children how to read, write, and master other skills. One of the most important skills, judging by the handmade tapestry overhead as well as the women in the photograph, was sewing. Chances are, this family was inadvertently training for their future in a new land. (Courtesy of Irene Tzivelekis.)

The handsome family pictured here was photographed in Athens before leaving for the United States. It is evident by his uniform that the man on the right is enrolled in the Greek army, being neither the breadwinner nor the youngest male of the family. Once the soldier's term was completed, they would head to New York to meet the rest of their family in Astoria. (Author's collection.)

ΒΑΣΙΛΕΙΟΝ ΤΗΣ ΕΛΛΑΔΟΣ

ΥΠΟΔ|ΣΙΣ ΧΩΡΙΚΗΣ ΛΕΡΟΥ

Αΰξ. ἀριθ. 3277

Ὑπουργεῖον
Κοιν. Προνοίας

ΟΜΑΣ ΑΙΜΑΤΟΣ

ὑπογραφὴ κατόχου

'Επώνυμον ΘΕΜΕΛΗ
"Ονομα Ἄννα
Πατρώνυμον Μιχαὴλ
"Ονομα συζύγου Χριστόδουλος
"Ονομα μητρὸς Εἰρήνη
Γένος Παπαδούλη
"Ετος γεννήσεως 1922
Τόπος γεννήσεως Λέρος
'Επάγγελμα Οἰκιακὰ
Τόπος κατοικίας Λέρος
Διεύθυνσις κατοικίας Ἁγ. Μαρίνα
Ὑπηκοότης Ἑλληνικὴ
Θρήσκευμα Χριστ: ὀρθόδοξος
"Ονομα Δήμου Λέρου
Αΰξ. ἀριθμός μητρώου 337
'Εν Λέρῳ τῇ 23ᵉ Φ/ρίου 1949
Ὁ ΔΙΟΙΚΗΤΗΣ ΥΠΟδ/σεως
Διοίκησης Ἰωάννη
ὑποδ/ρχος

Plans to leave Greece and travel to America required a great many things. Depending on financial stability, it was expected that multiple trips would be taken back and forth between one's village and Athens in order to secure passports and other important documents for every family member. This process took anywhere from a few months to a few years. This passport was secured in 1949, which may have been the year the process to leave began. (Courtesy of Irene Tzivelekis.)

Ἀκριβές ἀντίγραφον
ἐκ τοῦ πρωτοτύπου. —
Λέρος 25 - 6ᵉ Μαρτίου 1955
Διοικητὴς ὑποδ/σεως

Φούρλαρης Γρηγόριος
ὑποδ/ρχος

ΒΑΣΙΛΕΙΟΝ ΤΗΣ ΕΛΛΑΔΟΣ

ΔΕΛΤΙΟΝ
ΤΑΥΤΟΤΗΤΟΣ

ΤΗΣ

Ἄννης Θέμελη

BAΣIΛEION THΣ EΛΛAΔOΣ

ΔΙΟΙΚΗΣΙΣ ΧΩΡΟΦΥΛΑΚΗΣ Λέρου.

ΤΜΗΜΑ

Αΰξ. άριθ 554

'Υπογραφή Κατόχου

Ἐπώνυμον ΘΕΜΕΛΗΣ
'Ονομα Χριστόδουλος
Πατρώνυμον Πέτρος
'Ονομα συζύγου Άννα
'ονομα μητρός Χαριτωμένη.
Γένος
'Ετος Γεννήσεως 1911
Τόπος Γεννήσεως Πάτμος
'Επάγγελμα Ναυτικός
Τόπος κατοικίας Λέρος
Διεύθυνσις κατοικίας Εὐαγγελισμός
'Υπηκοότης Ἑλληνική ὁμογενή
Θρήσκευμα Χριστιανός ὀρθόδοξος
'Ονομα Δήμου Λέρου
Αΰξων άριθ. μητρώου 357
'Εν Λέρω τῇ 9/6/1947
Ο ΔΙΟΙΚΗΤΗΣ

This passport was reissued in 1947 in order to legally migrate this man's family to America. Word of the GI Bill and what it entailed led many Europeans, especially Greeks, to head for America in order to chase the "American Dream." In 1944, President Roosevelt was recorded saying, "I trust Congress will soon provide similar opportunities to members of the merchant marines who have risked their lives time and time again during the war for the welfare of the country." (Courtesy of Anna Feggaros.)

As early as the 1930s, many friendships were formed in neighborhoods as well as at churches throughout the Greek community. Here, friends gather by a pier in New York on a weekend excursion. (Courtesy of Lara Tewes.)

21

Many Greeks began to migrate to America during the 1950s, and several were likely to have booked passage on the Greek ship SS *Queen Frederica*, a troopship turned cruise ship. The journey from Piraeus, Athens, to New York Harbor took approximately two weeks. The *Queen Frederica* was named after the wife of King Paul of Greece. (Author's collection.)

The seven families pictured here keep up the tradition of potluck dinners. This was a way to bring Greeks together with people they would not otherwise meet, if they were members of different Greek Orthodox churches or societies within the community. (Courtesy of Sophia Kyriazis.)

Though most Greeks endured long journeys on ships such as the SS *Patricia* or SS *Queen Federica*, or through war, to arrive in New York, some had other means of arrival. According to an article in the *Bayside Times* dated May 26, 1955, some Greeks would arrive in New York under the "auspices of the Church World Service and the Intergovernmental Committee for European migration, pending that they had family and jobs waiting for them when they arrived." (Author's collection.)

Ellis Island remains one of the greatest symbols of a better life filled with opportunities and possibilities, the life-altering reason that most Europeans migrated to America. Arriving on Ellis Island was a breath of fresh air for Greeks who had seen their country torn apart by war and disaster time and time again. (Photograph by Stathoula Rozeas.)

The Statue of Liberty, the greatest symbol of freedom, was a sight for Greeks of all ages finally arriving in America. Having learned about her, many people still claim that it was much larger and grander than what they had imagined it to be. Here, Greeks would seek opportunity after opportunity to better their own and their family's standing. (Photograph by Stathoula Rozeas.)

Having used their means to bring their families to America, Greeks would hear their language spoken in passing or run into other Greeks in church every Sunday, and build friendships and relationships that would last their entire lives. These men are shown outside their new homes, in this case apartments, in New York in 1948. (Author's collection.)

Family members going into business together was often the only way immigrants knew to survive upon arrival in New York. No matter their financial standing or career lineage back in Greece, it was "back to the drawing board" after arriving in New York. Families worked whatever jobs they could and saved their pennies, making ends meet in order to invest in opportunities they could never have had before, such as their own "famous" New York shops, like the one pictured here. (Courtesy of Irene Tzivelekis.)

With a roof over their heads in New York, and having established American citizenship, folks could return to Greece and bring the rest of their family to their new home. Pictured here are women who were going to be reunited with their husbands, fathers, and brothers, and are saying their goodbyes to friends, until they meet again. (Courtesy of Irene Tzivelekis.)

For many Greeks, the move to Queens was the easiest one yet. In Astoria, family members would rent apartments close by and, in what would become Sunday traditions, walk with each other to the nearby churches and diners. Pictured here is a family finally reunited in Queens in the late 1950s, on their Astoria rooftop. The baby, the first family member born a US citizen, is being displayed proudly on her grandmother's lap. (Courtesy of Irene Papadoulis.)

The early 1960s was a beautiful time for recently established New Yorkers. Pictured here is one of the first holidays enjoyed by the entire family, and family friends, in an Astoria apartment. New friends were still arriving from Greece, needing guidance from those who already lived in America. Though the transition wasn't easy for anyone, it was a welcoming world for those who came after 1955. It looks as if it's the first course of a holiday dinner: traditional Greek salad and Kalamata olives are served first. (Courtesy of Irene Tzivelekis.)

Pictured here with a friend is Militsa Hatzidaki, a Greek folk singer who sang about the war. It was a family effort—her father wrote the songs, her mother composed, and Militsa performed them with her siblings. Though certain songs written by her father were never copyrighted, Militsa and her family, who hailed from the Dodecanese, never let it stop them from singing their own songs live. Seeing the Statue of Liberty was an accomplishment for anyone who was Greek, whether they lived in America or came to visit friends. (Courtesy of Anna Feggaros.)

The Empire State Building in Manhattan was another awesome sight for Greeks now living in America. People would pose for photographs at these sites and send them to Greece in order to show their extended family evidence of their new life and the awe-inspiring sights. Pictured here in the 1950s is a young Greek couple who met in New York and got married after discovering how much they had in common. This was the story for most Greeks, contrary to the popular belief that arranged marriages were the norm. (Courtesy of Frank Ginis.)

In the 1920s, many families who had migrated to the United States from Greece began to move to New York. Soon, families began to grow, both physically and financially, which bought a new phenomenon to many Greeks: homeownership. Moving into Astoria and communities as far as the Rockaways, many families like the Theodosious, pictured here, had truly attained the American dream. (Courtesy of Constantine E. Theodosiou.)

A first-generation Greek American girl is all dressed up and ready to go. Theodora is standing in front of her Woodside home in the late 1930s. By then, many Greek families were attending church services and Greek school programs in small offices, basements, or public schools. (Courtesy of Maria Caputo.)

Apartment buildings and businesses began to be acquired heavily by Greeks during the 1960s and early 1970s. Those who had not moved into the suburbs had stayed behind to maintain their newly owned homes, apartment buildings, and businesses, such as coffee shops. The building pictured here still stands in Astoria, on Thirty-second Street and Twenty-first Avenue. (Author's collection.)

Two young Greek boys stand in front of their family residence. This photograph was taken in February 1958 on Seventy-ninth Street in Jackson Heights. (Courtesy of Maria Caputo.)

A first-class Greek immigrant poses for the camera in the early 1920s. Stavroula Theodosiou was now called Stella because of the difficulty Americans had pronouncing her Greek name. She migrated to New York from Detroit's Greektown before the Great Depression. (Courtesy of Constantine E. Theodosiou.)

The Themelis women stand on their rooftop in Astoria, New York, in the early 1960s. The women posed for the camera in order for Mr. Themelis to work on his photography hobby. Also depicted are skills that Mrs. Themelis taught her daughter: sewing. The dresses they wear are handmade. (Courtesy of Irene Tzivelekis.)

In almost every Greek household, photographs and other ephemera, such as this map, are on display. The most valuable possessions that Greek immigrants bought to their new country were photographs and memories of the times prior to immigration. (Author's collection.)

A little Greek American girl stands in her Jackson Heights backyard. A pitched tent nearby means that these Greeks have finally taken to American pastimes, such as camping. In May 1972, the weather was warm enough to attempt camping for the first time at home before hitting the great outdoors. (Courtesy of Maria Caputo.)

The young man pictured here is serving his new country and achieving the dream of owning his first automobile. Many young men who immigrated to America had big goals and pushed to achieve their dreams. (Courtesy of Lara Tewes.)

By the early 1970s, Jackson Heights was another highly Greek-populated area. In this 1971 photograph, Kostas Makris holds his little niece in front of their abode. A new generation is already well underway within the Greek community. (Courtesy of Maria Caputo.)

Two

OLD WORLD INFLUENCES IN A BRAVE NEW WORLD

Shown here is a Greek American family standing at the park underneath the Hell Gate Bridge in Astoria. In June 1959, the bridge was still a wonder to look at. Conception of the bridge itself began in the early 1900s. It crosses the East River and had once been the longest steel-arch bridge in the world. Greek Americans still gather there today after the Greek Independence Day parade. (Courtesy of Irene Papadoulis.)

In the early 1950s, many Greek immigrants moved from Manhattan to Jackson Heights, thus expanding Little Greece a few extra miles. This photograph illustrates the changing community of Jackson Heights, with a view of the elevated tracks above this tight-knit family. (Courtesy of Stathoula Rozeas.)

Despite being in a new country filled with different opportunities, for Greek Americans, the essence of home remained the same. Mrs. Ginis and her family carry on with the routine of their day outdoors before they prepare dinner. (Courtesy of Stathoula Rozeas.)

Though some relatives stayed in Greece while others moved on, families never lost touch. Pictured here is Irene Maikou, one of the strong Greek women who kept her family in the old country stable and who kept in touch with the American relatives. (Author's collection.)

Family members gather at a new home in Astoria, Queens, in order to celebrate their family members' success in achieving the American dream. Grandparents, parents, and children often shared two rooms in one apartment in order to make ends meet and support each other financially. (Author's collection.)

OFFICIAL MEMBERSHIP BOOK
BROTHERHOOD OF PAINTERS, DECORATORS & PAPERHANGERS
OF AMERICA

SOCIAL SECURITY NO.   Card No.

076-96-4730   Receipts For Dues   962 762
                     and Assessments

Name... Chris THEMELIS

Type of Membership... BeN   Date Init. July 10-59

Initiated in L. U. 51   of   New York   N.Y.
                  No.   City   State

Date of Birth MAY 14-1911   Age at Initiation 118

Initiation Fee (Amount actually paid)... 75.00

                                    J. Thompson
President   Fin. Sec.
Local Union No. 848   of   N.Y.   N.Y.
                              City   State

Members must designate the name of beneficiary or change of beneficiary on blank provided on
preceding page which must be signed also by the Financial Secretary.

In many cases, men abandoned the professions they held in the old country in order to join the American workforce as laborers, as illustrated by the Painter's Union booklet pictured here. As indicated by the date, these are the jobs that were offered to immigrants when they arrived in America. (Author's collection.)

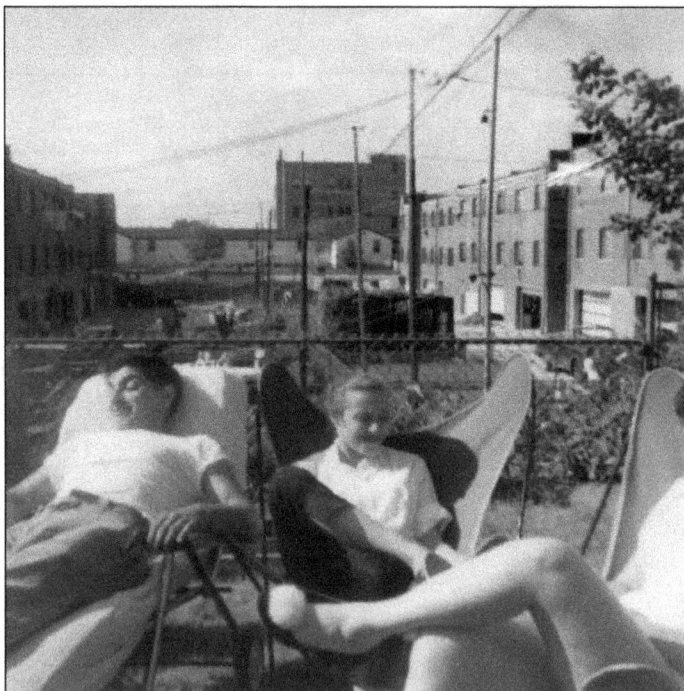

By the early 1960s, the Greek American community had their feet set firmly on the ground in their new country. First- and second-generation Greek Americans were born, routines were established, and opportunities to reach one's goals were everywhere. Here, a family gathers in the backyard of their Jackson Heights home. (Courtesy of Maria Caputo.)

When a family unit moved to New York, they often sent letters to their extended family back in Greece to keep them informed of what was going on and of everyone's new life. Before the age of the Internet, letters often took upwards of two weeks to be delivered, so the correspondence between family members took one month in totality. Oftentimes, a family would send photographs of what was going on and write a little note on the back of them, like the photograph above, which was sent in December 1952. Based on the words on the back (below), it was sent to a home where only the mother and daughter resided while the father was in America preparing for his family's journey to the land of freedom. (Courtesy of Anna Feggaros.)

In this photograph, brothers-in-law sit in front of one of the statues of a Byzantine bird in Central Park. According to Sara Cedar Miller at the Central Park Conservancy, "There are eight of them [eagles] at the Zoo facing the seal pond, near 64th street behind the brick Arsenal building." (Courtesy of Irene Tzivelekis.)

Education began in the home, as is illustrated in this photograph. Mother and daughter sit outside their Jackson Heights home, toys scattered on the ground. Among the toys is a cash register, to encourage the little girl's possible interest in business. (Courtesy of Maria Caputo.)

Oftentimes, Greeks found themselves not only in a war against other countries, but battling Mother Nature herself. Earthquakes and other natural disasters devastated communities, forcing them to rebuild. These photographs show the calamity of one of the worst earthquakes, in Kalamata, Greece, in the 1980s. Greek Americans did all they could to support their devastated families back home. (Courtesy of Chris Rozeas.)

Though the majority of the flourishing Greek community moved from the borough of Manhattan to Queens between the late 1950s and mid-1960s, people still returned to their old neighborhood to visit family on the weekends and shop for groceries and other items. This photograph captures the essence of this life: a family with a first-generation Greek American, baby William Ginis, going about their weekend routine. (Courtesy of Frank Ginis.)

The Makris kids have assimilated to American pastimes like basketball. This 1972 photograph was taken just before the kids dribbled and shot a few hoops. (Courtesy of Maria Caputo.)

Leaving Greece meant leaving behind a varied standard of living, including war, family life, and social routines. Greeks now living in New York would make do with home visits and the occasional excursion to neighboring beaches. These pictures indicate how a family might have spent quality time in Greece and, in the New World, projecting deep-rooted homesickness by spending a day in Coney Island. Judging by the filled beach scene in the background, beautiful days like this brought the Greek community together, encouraging them to make the journey safely from Queens to southern Brooklyn, complete with a picnic lunch, to remember what life was like in the old country. (Courtesy of Frank Ginis.)

According to the testimonies of many Greeks who were the first to migrate into Queens, women were not expected to stay in the home. In many cases, they were encouraged to leave the confines of the home to pursue an educational career or broaden their skills. Sewing, for example, might allow a woman like Maria Ginis, pictured here, to pursue a job as a seamstress, fashioning anything from *fezes* (red hats) to society women's outfits like the one she is shown wearing. (Courtesy of Frank Ginis.)

In this 1950s photograph, an apartment in Astoria, Queens, is filled with family, friends, and music. Such a scene could be found on almost every day of the week. It was not out of the ordinary in a Greek home for talented musicians to pass down their skills to the upcoming generations, and for grandparents to pass down stories of their family and life in the old country to their grandchildren. Three generations of family and friends are gathered here, enjoying music and company. (Courtesy of Irene Tzivelekis.)

In this photograph, the beginnings of a band are having a practice and teaching a little girl the melodies of the songs they grew up with. The man at center holds a *bouzouki*, a popular instrument dating back to ancient Greece that gained in popularity with Greek folk songs throughout time. (Courtesy of Anna Feggaros.)

Sweet sixteens were a new concept to the Greek population. Greeks had always mainly celebrated a child's nameday on a grander scale than a birthday. A nameday is based on the religious tradition of a saint's feast day: a child is named after a certain saint, and thereafter celebrates that saint's feast day. Since children are almost always named after their grandparents, this maintains strong family and religious traditions. This photograph is an example of a new-world influence in a traditional Greek American family. (Courtesy of Stathoula Rozeas.)

Hardworking Greek families were frugal, keeping their finances in order. Their ultimate goal upon arriving in America was to secure for their children a good education and to give them the opportunity to purchase a home—and their own goal was to do the same. In this 1920s photograph, Nicholas Papazisimos poses for the camera. He migrated to the United States from Greece, but he moved to Rockaway from Indiana. He owned a shoe store, thus accomplishing one part of the American dream. (Courtesy of Constantine E. Theodosiou.)

Young families never veered far from their old-world routines. Here, a family is on their way to Holy Cross Greek Orthodox Church in Whitestone, on a beautiful morning, dressed in their Sunday best. (Courtesy of Frank Ginis.)

Any given celebration provided an excuse for extended families and friends in the Greek American community to get together. In this photograph, a group gathers to witness one of the first large snowfalls any of them had experienced, in February 1961. Astoria Park was absolutely covered in snow, a sight completely foreign to Greek Americans in their mother country. (Author's collection.)

Assembled in front of an Astoria apartment building, the Themelis family and bridal party gather for their first Greek "family wedding" since moving to New York. Old world meets new, as grandparents look on at the bride and her bridal party, complete with flower girl and ring bearer, customs that Greeks adopted upon moving to America. (Courtesy of Irene Tzivelekis.)

45

Family and friends gather in Jackson Heights before going to a church event. In April 1962, families within the Greek community began to grow, spurring more family oriented events. (Courtesy of Stathoula Rozeas.)

This photograph shows a Greek family doing what they do best: socializing over dinner. Children were not even segregated from the table. Photographed in April 1957, this family was likely talking about ways to help out their relations in Greece, or who would be next arriving in America. (Courtesy of Frank Ginis.)

This 1960s photograph shows a trio of siblings, first-generation Americans, visiting a candy store and indulging in some treats. The children are probably on their way home from Sunday school, based on their attire. Sunday school in the Greek Orthodox church consists of a kind of religious class time that takes place during mass, to teach young children religion and what is taking place during mass that day. (Courtesy of William Ginis.)

Dr. and Mrs. Papageorgiou dance together at an event taking place in Crystal Palace. Dr. Papageorgiou had come to the United States to study medicine after serving in the US army. Eventually, he moved his medical office from Park Avenue to Ditmars Boulevard to be closer to his friends and family. (Courtesy of Anna Feggaros.)

Crystal Palace hosted Greek events from its grand opening in 1955 until closing its doors in 2007. Located at 31-09 Broadway in Astoria, Crystal Palace had been Skouras Theaters until it was purchased by the Kalamaras brothers. (Courtesy of Irene Tzivelekis.)

THE PARTHENON MARBLES IN EXILE

Throughout their history in America, many Greeks have sent financial help to their families and various organizations back in Greece, to aid their hometowns and villages and preserve their culture. An example of a philanthropic cause close to the heart of Greek Americans is shown in this flier, acquired from the Parthenon. (Author's collection.)

Pictured here is part of the Omogenia pages of the *Ethniko Kirika*, translated roughly as *The National Herald*. Since 1915, the *Herald* carried news from Greece to America. Now also online, it has been found to encourage younger generations to keep abreast of goings-on in the Greek American world. *The National Herald* was preceded by *The Atlantis* paper, which was founded by the Greek Vlastos brothers in the 1890s. These periodicals covered, and still do cover, major events like wars and war relief efforts. (Author's collection.)

The weekends usually brought together people of all ages. A group of friends gathers in a Queens backyard, socializing over soda-pop, something that was new to immigrants to America. For many immigrants, seeing a television set and, eventually, owning one were dreams in and of themselves. (Courtesy of Lara Tewes.)

Transportation to and from Greece was very difficult until the 1980s, when even some of Greece's islands built airports just to accommodate small airlines such as Olympic Airways. This made it easier for Greeks to travel back and forth to America and secure the well-being of their family and friends. The handwritten note below explains that the plane shown above arrived at the new airport in Leros, Dodecanese, on June 13, 1984, and that the unusual sight had drawn a huge crowd. (Author's collection.)

A little girl sits outside of a 1930s Manhattan shop, just as many children may have done back in Greece. The Greek community found a multitude of opportunities in the big city before moving into Little Greece, Astoria. (Courtesy of Lara Tewes.)

A young man and woman stand outside their first home in the United States, which in many cases was an apartment. Taking photographs was a way for Greek Americans to remember what they'd accomplished. Before heading over to a relative's house in Astoria, a Greek pastime of coffee in the afternoon wasn't forgotten. Since coffee shops were not all the rage in Queens in the early 1930s, visiting friends and relatives with a sweet treat was a popular routine. (Courtesy of Lara Tewes.)

Central Park stands proud and beautiful in this 1930s photograph. The park was one of the locations where many Greeks would gather to socialize and catch up on news before moving into Queens. Having been used to being outdoors, Greek Americans found Central Park to be the ultimate meeting place. (Courtesy of Lara Tewes.)

The sight of the world's fair under construction was something that struck a lot of excitement into American hearts, especially Greeks. The preview was photographed, and all of New York, especially Queens, looked on until opening day, to see what the future had in store for them. (Courtesy of Lara Tewes.)

Friends gather in front of the site of the 1939 world's fair in Queens, waiting to glimpse the future. The Greek community had something more to write home about. (Courtesy of Lara Tewes.)

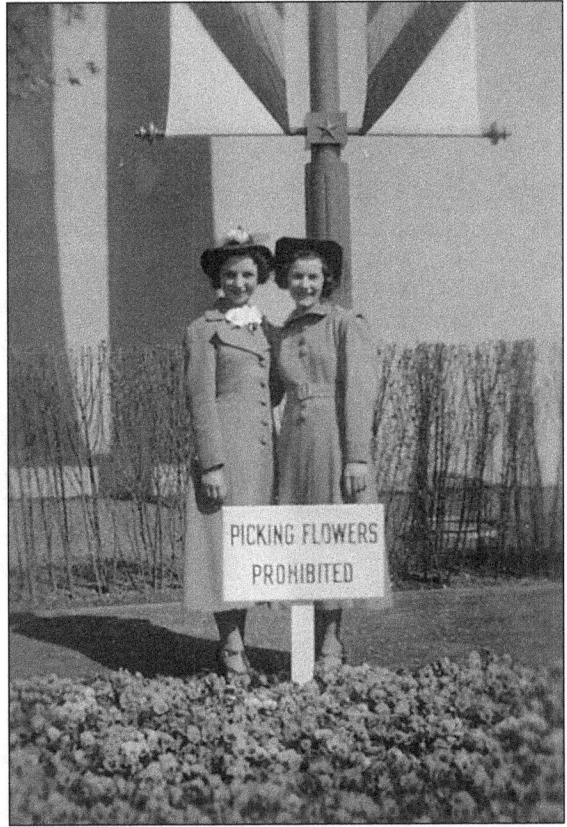

Crowds of all races and backgrounds gather at the doors, waiting to see the world's fair in Queens. In 1939, many Greeks and people of all backgrounds gathered in the World's Fair Marina in order to view new-world wonders and pavilions dedicated to each country. This building marked the main entrance to the fair. (Courtesy of Lara Tewes.)

One thing Greeks brought to America with them was their love of socializing. When incorporated into one's line of work, the doors were magically opened. Here stands Frank Ginis (center, holding tray), serving Manhattan's elite in the late 1950s. He migrated from Greece in the early 1950s and almost immediately rubbed elbows with America's finest. (Courtesy of Frank Ginis.)

Three

GREEK ORTHODOX CHURCHES AND SCHOOLS

Upon arrival in Queens, word of mouth among the Greeks led them to involvement in the community, especially with the church. Shown here is a scene in St. Markella Greek Orthodox Church, located on Twenty-sixth Street in Astoria. Opening its doors in 1954, a small congregation raised their families and nurtured their community from this church, founded under *Despoti* or His Eminence, Metropolitan Petros of Astoria. (Author's collection.)

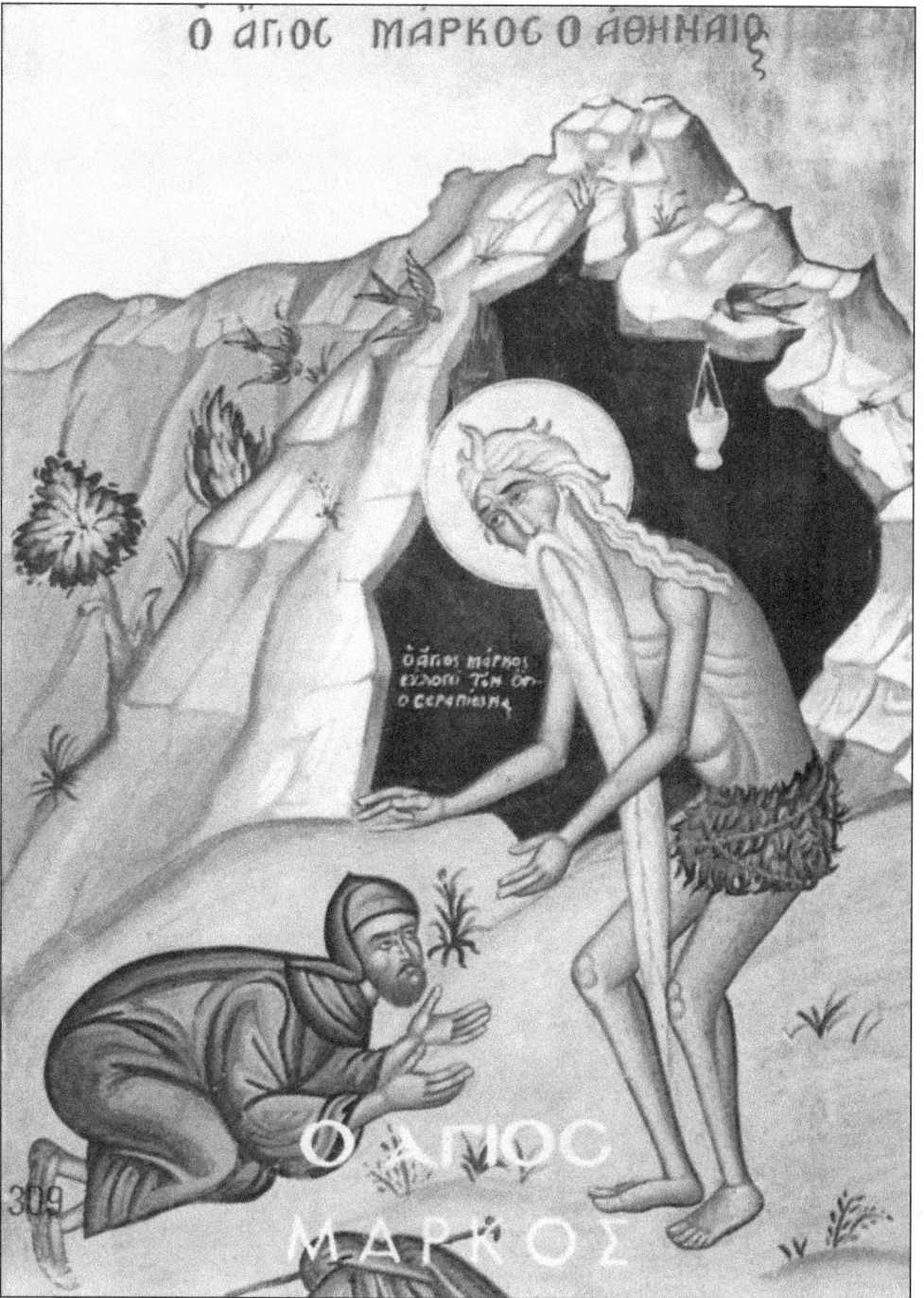

This is an example of religious booklets that were given out to parishioners and, especially, Sunday school students. This was not only a historical work about the plight of saints and religious holidays, but also told a heavily religious story that was necessary in order to keep the Greek Orthodox religion a staple in the minds and hearts of first-generation Greek Americans. The booklet pictured, about St. Marcus the Athenian, is an example of those found in the Greek American home. (Author's collection.)

This baptismal certificate dated January 21, 1923, like so many others, would be carried to the New World as proof of the brave people who came before present-day Greek Americans. This one in particular indicates that a couple from the island of Leros baptized their daughter Anna—who was just a little over one year old—with godmother Julia Kasti. (Author's collection.)

This photograph, also taken in St. Markella Greek Orthodox Church, shows an example of a community in a church setting built from the ground up. The Greek Orthodox community is still alive and thriving because of its faith and religious background. In the center, with the white beard and crown, is His Eminence Metropolitan Petros of Astoria, who founded St. Markella in 1954. The Metropolis now consists of multiple churches and several monasteries. To the immediate left stands the future His Eminence Metropolitan Pavlos. (Author's collection.)

While glancing over the academic schedule at a Greek Orthodox day school, it is not uncommon to find such classes as religion, Greek history, Greek mythology, and the like. Among after-school activities, Greek folk dancing was one of those most sought after by parents, in order to keep their children knowledgeable about their past. (Author's collection.)

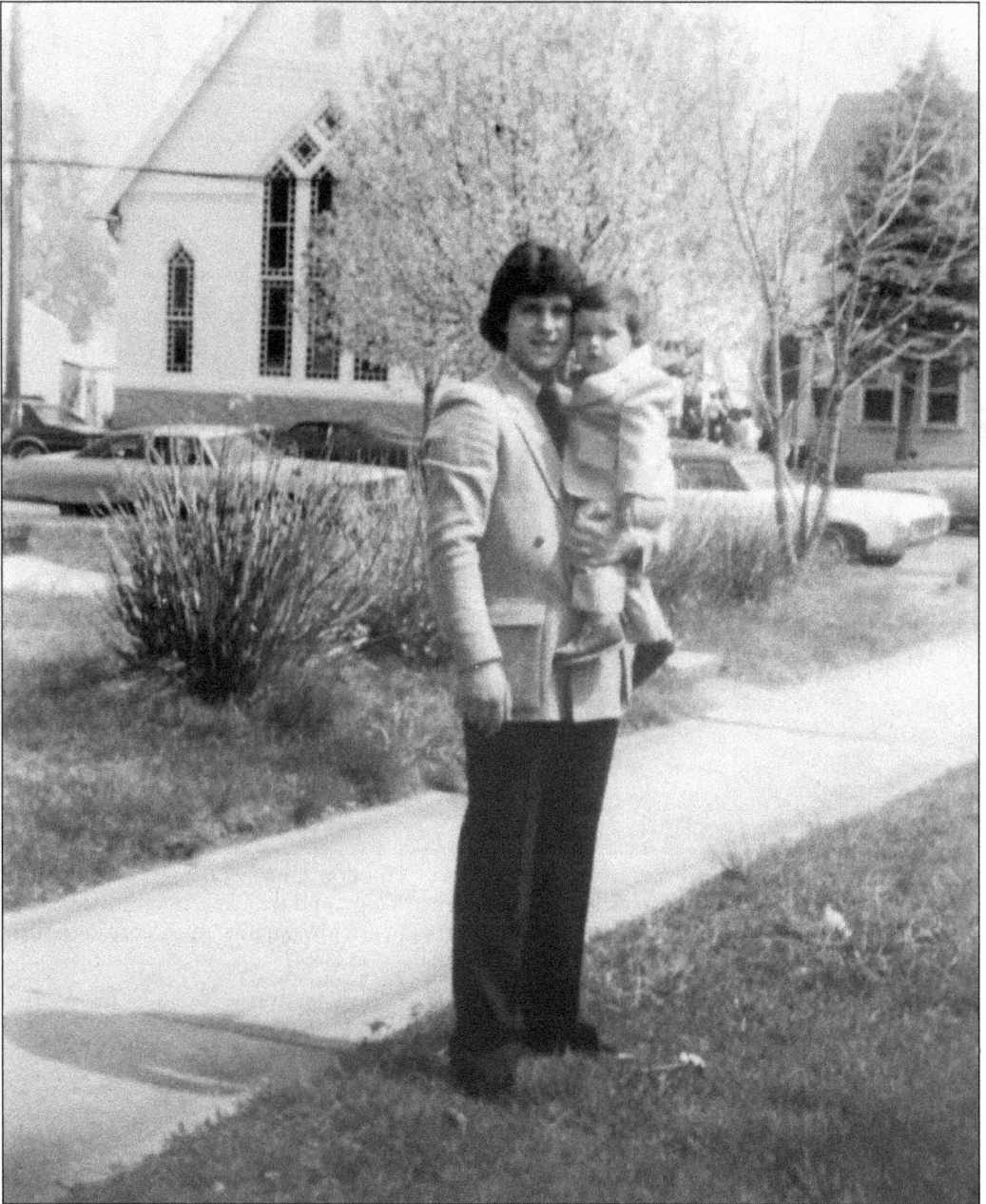

This photograph, taken in Whitestone just a few steps away from Holy Cross Greek Orthodox Church, shows a father taking his son to church. Greek Americans often introduce their children to the church at a very early age to preserve Greek religious backgrounds and histories. (Courtesy of John Rozeas.)

In this late 1950s photograph, His Eminence Metropolitan Petros of Astoria looks over his congregation as his grandnephew, who is now His Eminence Metropolitan Pavlos of North and South America, stands to his right. The Greek Orthodox Church of St. Markella was once a small building, as is the one in the photograph, and grew as the community grew. Members of the community also helped out during services, as is evident by the man in the suit to the left of His Eminence Metropolitan Petros. (Author's collection.)

This Greek American family, dressed in their best, gathers in front of their Queens residence. The Makris family was on their way to a christening in August 1960. Three generations are shown in this photograph, and the youngest child is a first-generation Greek American. This is an example of family and friends gathered in order to welcome a new generation of Greek Americans. (Courtesy of Maria Caputo.)

As was the tradition back in Greece, Sunday school became a huge part of a Greek American child's life. In this photograph, a mother (along with her sister) picks up her little girl from Sunday school. Anna and Stella Papadoulis walked hand-in-hand through the streets, from church to their home. Greece had only recently come out of slavery and World War II. Citizens of the islands were raised in fear of dictators and experienced the daily threat of death practically knocking at village doors. At the time this photograph was taken, around 1950, life could be navigated safely, and a child's education once again came first. (Courtesy of Irene Tzivelekis.)

This photograph, taken in Kalamata, Greece, shows how important school was even in the early 1950s. The school bus has pulled over to usher the children out and into the arms of their families, who lived in a village so small that everyone knew everyone else. One can tell by the fields in the background that Kalamata was not yet an up and coming town, making more important to the male youths the value of education, work, and community in order to secure a brighter future. (Courtesy of Chris Rozeas.)

Having Sunday school as a basis, many first-generation Greek American students walked to and from their day schools with friends they'd met. Lifelong friendships were plentiful in those days; common ground could be established from the surprise of hearing one's native tongue spoken on the streets. Finding someone who originated from the same Greek city, village, or island was indeed a rare thing until, beginning in the 1930s, associations began to disseminate such information. Pictured here is an example of such a friendship. (Courtesy of Stathoula Rozeas.)

Meeting other Greeks sprouted many new friendships in Queens public schools. Frequently, these friendships would last a lifetime. Pictured here is a group of Greek Orthodox children outside of Long Island City High School. The Greek culture has always fascinated others. (Courtesy of Frank Ginis.)

The first-generation Greek American community had high graduation rates, including from private Greek schools such as St. Demetrios. This school's class of 1987 is pictured here. After high school, a large percentage of the community's students went off to college. Counselors, psychiatrists, doctors, and lawyers became well known throughout the Greek community, especially with the help of advertisements through Greek newspapers and television and radio stations. The Greek community's strong roots in America were firmly planted by the mid-1980s. (Courtesy of Lucy Argyros.)

William Spyropoulos Greek-American School of St. Nicholas in Flushing stands high on the academic excellence list as well, always teaching its students about their history. Here, the Evzones, or presidential guard, takes time out to visit some students as part of their enrichment program, which began in 1977. (Courtesy of Anna Feggaros.)

WILLIAM SPYROPOULOS
GREEK-AMERICAN DAY SCHOOL
of St. Nicholas Greek Orthodox Church, Flushing, N.Y.

ΣΟΦΟΚΛΕΟΥΣ

"ΑΝΤΙΓΟΝΗ"

Παρουσιαζει η Ογδοη ταξη του σχολειου,
με συμμετοχη των μαθητριων της
εβδομης ταξης.

Το εργο διδαξε η Κα Πεππη Βολικα

Υποβολεας: η Κα Ελενη Κεηπους

2 Ιουνιου 1995

The extraordinary educational system of the Greek American private schools is illustrated by the content of this flier: the eighth-graders of William Spyropoulos reciting, in ancient Greek, Sophocles's tragedy *Antigone*. (Author's collection.)

In this 1965 photograph, members of a church congregation gather for a picnic. These gatherings would be the springboard for church festivals, which would benefit the church and, in turn, keep the community united. Here is a vibrant Greek community, having a picnic in Queens during a turbulent time in American history. Thankfully, many families remained intact and stronger than ever, regardless of what was going on in other countries. (Courtesy of Frank Ginis.)

A crowd begins to gather before a baptism in St. Markella, now complete after having been rebuilt following an accidental fire in the late 1990s. It was a miracle that no one was hurt. The Greek community quickly began to raise funds in order to restore their church. Even younger members held community events and helped in any way they thought possible. (Author's collection.)

Retired painter, avid artist, and photographer Christodoulos Themelis takes on the old tradition of fashioning palm leaves into a cross in the early 1990s. The palm crosses were always fashioned on church grounds, and by other members of the community, just in time for Palm Sunday. On the holiday, these palm crosses and more would be passed out to churchgoers to remember the Sunday that Jesus entered Jerusalem after having brought Lazarus back from the dead. (Author's collection.)

St. Catherine's and St. George's Church, located on Thirty-third Street, is affiliated with St. Demetrios Church and has been rebuilt recently. It is still one of the most beautiful churches in Astoria. (Courtesy of St. Demetrios Greek Orthodox Church.)

In the early 1930s, afternoon Greek school was held in the church office, and classes took place in PS 122. Finally, September 1957 brought the long-anticipated St. Demetrios Day School opening, with students from kindergarten through eighth grade in attendance. Approximately 250 students were enrolled on the first day. (Courtesy of St. Demetrios Greek Orthodox Church.)

Greek heritage was not only preserved, but now was becoming even more important. In 1927, the cornerstone of St. Demetrios Greek Orthodox Church was laid, and in 1928, the church opened its doors for its first service. This community grew with each passing year, despite the Great Depression, and eventually came to surround not only Jamaica, but areas as far away as Bellerose. Today, St. Demetrios is still an iconic part of not only the Greek community, but the greater Astoria and Queens communities as well. (Courtesy of St. Demetrios Greek Orthodox Church.)

Saint Irene Chrysovalantou, located on Ditmars Boulevard in Queens, is a licensed day-care center that reaches out to families in need. (Author's collection.)

Transfiguration of Christ Greek Orthodox Church, located on Ninety-eighth Street in Corona, has been a staple of the Greek Community since it opened its doors with services on Palm Sunday 1958. Jackson Heights was also heavily populated by Greeks in the 1950s, which is why meetings were held in St. Demetrios, in Astoria, to push for the building of Transfiguration of Christ Church. (Author's collection.)

Though there are Greek Orthodox private schools scattered throughout Queens, with levels ranging from kindergarten to high school, there are also programs specifically dedicated to the study of Greek history. Queens College began the Center for Byzantine and Modern Greek Studies in 1974, under the guidance and dedication of director Harry Psomiades, pictured here giving a student an award. The center is an important educational mecca of the Greek community, then and now. (Courtesy of the Center for Byzantine and Modern Greek Studies in Queens College.)

St. Nicholas Greek Orthodox Church and William Spyropoulos School, located in Flushing, are still flourishing today. The huge property was recently able to accommodate an expansion to better serve the growing Greek community. (Author's collection.)

In this photograph, a talented young man poses with his guitar and piano. Self-taught students would often go from home to home, teaching other students various musical instruments, or, later, open their own schools in order to teach future generations songs and instruments to keep their history alive. (Courtesy of Lara Tewes.)

St. Irene's Church, located on Twenty-third Avenue in Astoria, has stood in the same location since 1972. There is not one Greek in Queens who does not know the story of the "Crying Icon" of the Virgin Mary and Baby Jesus that resides within St. Irene's (Author's collection.)

The most recent change to a church in the Greek Orthodox community of Queens was the remodeling of Holy Cross Greek Orthodox Church of Whitestone, and Holy Cross Greek Orthodox Day School, which it now faces. (Author's collection.)

Four

TRADITIONS
AND FESTIVITIES

Musicians of all ages did not give up on their passions when they arrived to start their new life in New York. The Athenian Guitar and Bouzoukee School, pictured here, is an example of the Greeks having never walked away from their crafts. (Author's collection.)

Family back in Greece, and people of all ages, like the group pictured here, were overjoyed to find out that New York granted them such respect as to celebrate their Independence Day in America. (Author's collection.)

In America, it became a custom for children of Greek descent to dress up in folk costumes on certain holidays, such as when marching in the Greek Independence Day parade. Pictured here is a girl wearing an *Amalia*, which was worn in the Peloponnese, and became a sort of national costume for Greek women. (Courtesy of Stathoula Rozeas.)

The *foustanella*, like the one pictured here, is the national costume for men of Greece. Named after the white skirt, it was historically worn by warriors and is what you will likely see if you run into an *evzone*, which is a member of the presidential guard. (Courtesy of Stathoula Rozeas.)

The first Greek parades did not take place in New York. This March 25 parade is in Kalamata, Greece, around 1962. The first Greek Independence Day celebrations in New York took place in City Hall Park around the 1890s. (Courtesy of Chris Rozeas.)

Many Greeks experienced their first Greek Independence Day parade in the United States at a young age, especially if it coincided with their year of arrival in New York. Pictured here in 1958, women and their children gather in Manhattan to watch the goings-on and to remember the bravery of the land from which they came. (Author's collection.)

The Ginis siblings stand at the el, waiting for the train to pick them up following the Greek Independence Day parade, in April 1965. They were heading back to their home, but not before getting off at the Ditmars station in order to continue festivities with friends and family in Astoria. (Courtesy of William Ginis.)

One of the biggest celebrations of the year for a Greek is Easter Sunday, when the entire family gathers around a lamb roasting on a spit in the backyard. In the 1960s, all backyards in Astoria were transformed into miniature versions of Greece. Along with the lamb roasting, other Greek delicacies were being prepared with love, such as *magiritsa* (varied lamb parts including intestines) and *frikase* (escarole and beef tenderloins, or any kind of meat the family enjoys). (Courtesy of Irene Tzivelekis.)

In this photograph, shot at an angle to capture the sight of a first Greek Easter in their Queens backyard, a family makes the final preparations before sharing in the traditional meal of roasted lamb on a spit. Extended family and friends of every background are always invited to big feasts. (Courtesy of Irene Tzivelekis.)

All Greek Orthodox holidays result in the community gathering together, as shown here. Priests are invited to commence the event with a blessing and a prayer. The community comes together and traditions are kept intact; everyone discusses religious and historic aspects of each event or holiday. (Author's collection.)

In this photograph, a little boy gets hands-on training when it comes to building the traditional spit to prepare the Easter Sunday feast. He will one day pass the custom down to his family. (Courtesy of Stathoula Rozeas.)

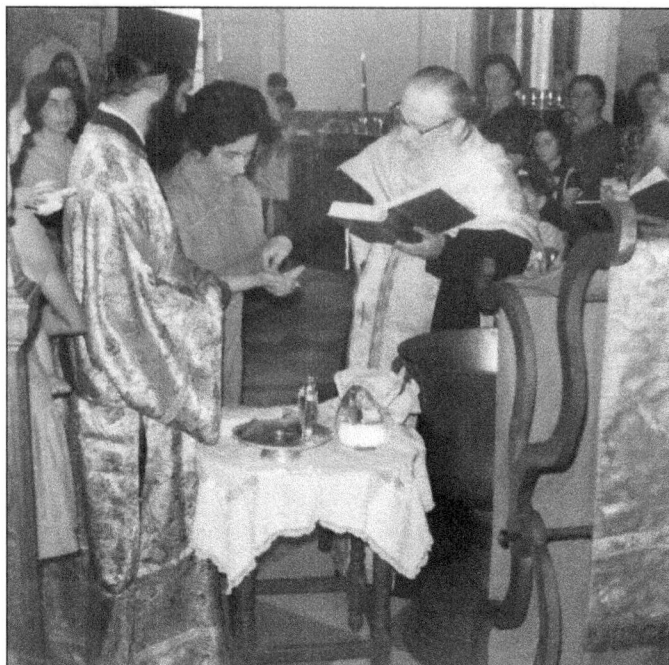

Another major event in a Greek's life is their baptism. Usually performed when the child is under the age of three, the ceremony involves the child's godparents (who were the main witnesses, or *koumbari*, in the child's parents' marriage) reciting a few prayers over the child. Then, the child is expelled of Satan and is immersed three times in water, to be cleansed so that he or she can serve Christ. (Courtesy of Chris Rozeas.)

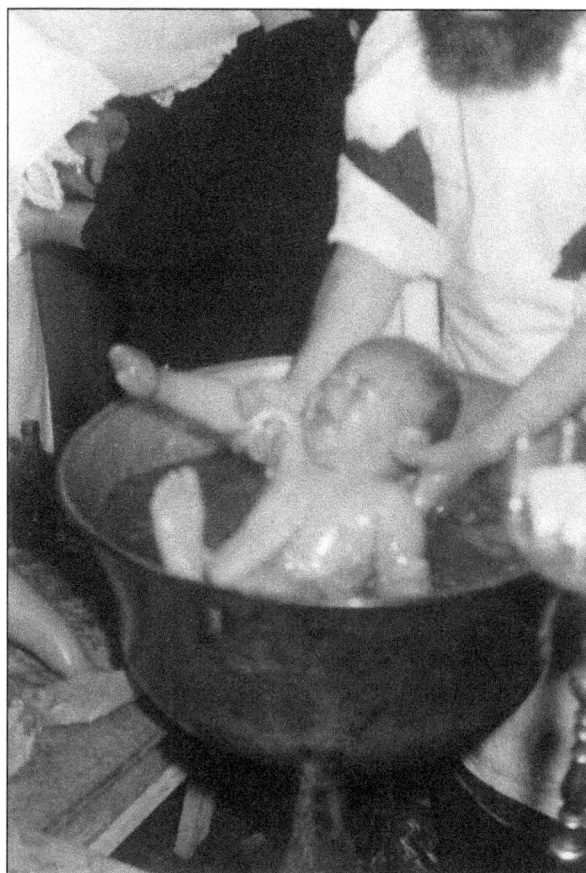

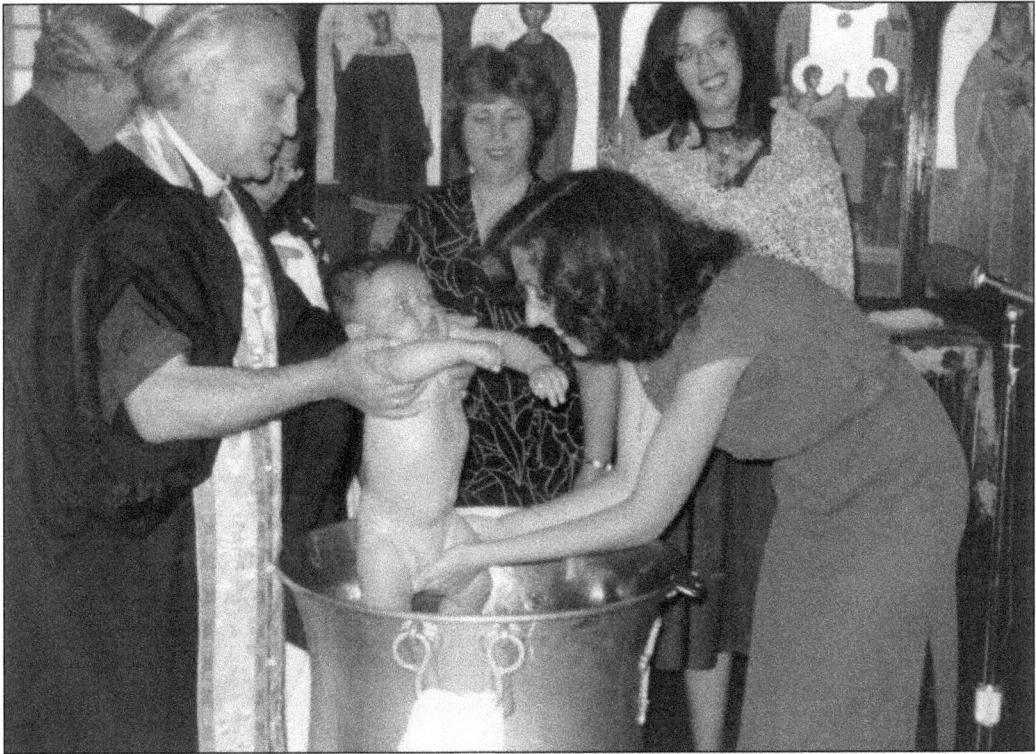

The godparents anoint the entire body of the baby with olive oil, which symbolizes that the grip of sin will slip right off. Greek Orthodox religion states that the original sin, Eve eating the apple from the tree, stays with a child until their baptism. (Courtesy of Stathoula Rozeas.)

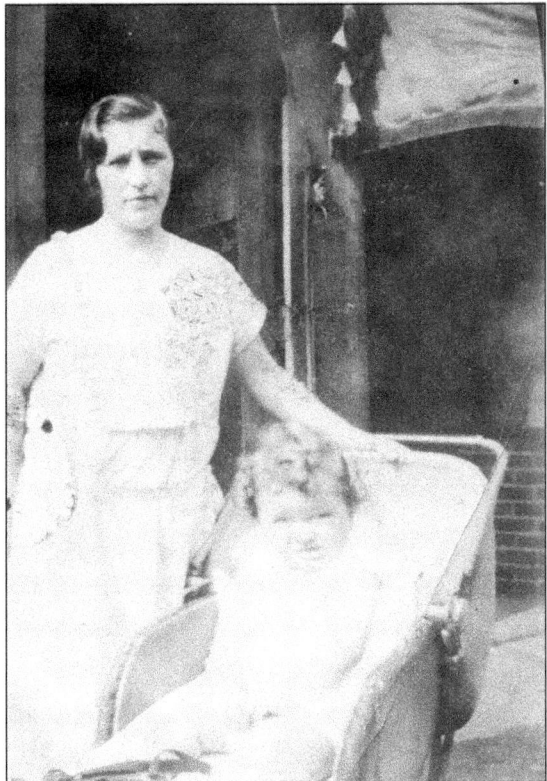

In this photograph from the 1930s, the Theodosiou baby is now wearing brand-new white clothing, as does every baby following their baptism. The post-baptismal baby is now a servant of God and is the center of attention at the ensuing celebration of this new life. (Courtesy of Constantine E. Theodosiou.)

Churchgoers in Jackson Heights, Queens, are all dressed up in order to attend a life-event, such as a wedding or baptism. Both events have always been huge in the life of a Greek, and it is customary for attendees to bring a gift for the person who the celebration is honoring, in order to usher in their new life. (Courtesy of Stathoula Rozeas.)

A *themelio*, or blessing of the church ground and cornerstone, takes place in the 1950s at St. Catherine's and George's Greek Orthodox Church. The priests and various members of the church and Greek Orthodox community gather to pray for the future church during this momentous occasion. (Courtesy of St. Demetrios.)

Beautiful floral arrangements adorn any Greek Orthodox church during the Easter holy week. The flowers on display surround Jesus on the cross, Mary, and John the Apostle, waiting to signify the resurrection. (Author's collection.)

Living in their new environments did not divert Greeks from their traditional holiday customs. Here, a family gathers at their new homestead in Whitestone, in celebration of the birth of Jesus Christ. Greeks who follow the New Testament celebrate Christmas on December 25, while Greeks who attend churches that follow Old Testament teachings and dating systems gather to celebrate on January 6. (Courtesy of Anna Feggaros.)

Friends and members of Greek associations would visit heavily Greek-populated neighborhoods in Queens to sing *kalanta* (Christmas carols). This custom is still strongly encouraged in Greece today, and one that children attending Greek Orthodox day schools are still taught. (Courtesy of Irene Tzivelekis.)

The soldier in this photograph was lost to his family in the early 1930s. Religiously and culturally, a memorial service for those who have passed away is customary in order for those left behind to remember the past. (Author's collection.)

ΙΕΡΑ ΜΟΝΗ
ΟCΙΑC ΕΙΡΗΝΗC ΧΡΥCΟΒΑΛΛΑΝΤΟΥ
ΛΥΚΟΒΡΥCΙC ΑΤΤΙΚΗC
Τ. ΘΥΓΙC 603 Κ.Τ.Α.

Τῇ 25- 8- 1972

Ἀρ. Πρωτ. . . . .

Πνευματικόν μου τέκνον   Ἄννα

Χαίρετε ἐν Κυρίῳ πάντοτε.

Ἡ χάρις τοῦ Παναγάθου Θεοῦ καὶ τῆς Ὁσίας Μητρὸς ἡμῶν Εἰρήνης Χρυσοβαλάντου εἴη ἀεὶ μεθ' ὑμῶν.

Ἔλαβον τὴν ἐπιστολήν σας *[handwritten text]*

Εὐχόμεθα ἐκ βάθους καρδίας ὅπως ἡ Θαυματουργὸς Χάρις τῆς Ἁγίας μας σᾶς ἐπισκιάζῃ πάντοτε καὶ εἰσακούῃ τῶν αἰτήσεών σας ἐνισχύουσα ὑμᾶς ψυχικῶς καὶ σωματικῶς καὶ παρέχουσα συγχρόνως τὴν ποθητὴν ὑγείαν καὶ διηνεκῆ εἰρήνην ψυχῆς καὶ ἀγαλλίασιν. Ἡ δὲ εὐλογία αὐτῆς εἴη διάχυτος ἐν τῷ οἴκῳ ὑμῶν.

Ἐντὸς τῆς ἐπιστολῆς μας σᾶς ἔχομεν τεμάχιον ἐκ τῶν εὐλογηθέντων μήλων τῆς Θαυματουργοῦ Ἁγίας μας, τὸ ὁποῖον λαμβάνετε μετὰ ἀπὸ τριῶν ἡμερῶν νηστεία ἀπὸ ἔλαιον παρακαλοῦντες ἐν προσευχῇ τὴν χάριν Αὐτῆς ὅπως τύχητε τῆς θείας ἀντιλήψεώς Της.

Μετ' εὐχῶν καὶ εὐλογιῶν
Ἡ πνευματικὴ Σας Μητέρα
Ἡγουμένη
Μελετία Μοναχὴ
Σταυροφόρος τοῦ Παν. Τάφου.

This letter is an example, sent by a family to a church, of a request for a memorial service. It is from the family of the deceased man shown on the previous page. Memorial services are religiously what help put the soul at peace and in a better position before God, and help illustrate to the community the impact that spirit had on a family's life. (Author's collection.)

Five

CELEBRATIONS AND THE COMMUNITY

A young girl poses for a photograph in front of the Triborough Bridge. Such photographs would be sent to family members back in Greece, many of whom were captivated by New York's bridges. (Courtesy of Irene Tzivelekis.)

Another realization of the American dream was running a successful business, like this Astoria shop pictured in the early 1950s. (Author's collection.)

The establishment of new friendships in New York become easier as Greeks introduced one other during *xorosperides*, or dances, such as the one shown here. (Author's collection.)

In this photograph, Greek folk singer Militsa Hatzidaki attends an event of the Lerian Association of New York. Here, in one of her many visits to the city, she stands with Lerian Association president Petros Proios, to her left. (Courtesy of Anna Feggaros.)

Greek celebrities continued to visit their friends and family in America, especially in New York. By the time Nikos Xanthopoulos (second from the left) visited Astoria, he was a legendary actor in the Greek movie industry. He starred in his first film in 1958 and immediately stole the hearts of Greek and Greek American girls alike. (Author's collection.)

A postcard advertising a movie starring the most beloved actress in all of Greece, Aliki Vouyiouklaki, and actor Demetris Papamichael, is an example of another much-loved Greek American pastime: taking in a Greek feature film at a local cinema. Though Skouras Theaters was also very popular, Manolides Theaters presented this film. It was one of the 16 films that Vouyiouklaki and Papamichael collaborated on during their marriage. After the couple's 1974 divorce, Vouyiouklaki continued to pursue acting roles and visit fans in New York. (Author's collection.)

ΑΛΙΚΗ ΒΟΥΓΙΟΥΚΛΑΚΗ
ΔΗΜΗΤΡΗΣ ΠΑΠΑΜΙΧΑΗΛ

PRESENTED BY:
MANOLIDES FILMS
2255 31TH ST. - ASTORIA - N. Y. - TEL. 932.9744

As can be seen in this 1950s photograph, the wedding celebration had yet to take on today's standards as the bridesmaids pose, smiling for the portrait. It is likely that, with a little help from each other, these dresses were designed and sewn by these beautiful women themselves. (Courtesy of Stathoula Rozeas.)

A couple joining hands in holy matrimony stands before the priest and underneath the *stefana* (wedding crowns), which represent the couple becoming one, at the beginning of their new life together. (Courtesy of Irene Tzivelekis.)

The entire bridal party and family smile for the camera, as the stefana are proudly displayed over the bridegroom's head, being held by the *koumbaro*, or male sponsor. The stefana are symbols that the young couple are now bonded in holy matrimony, and the koumbaro, or male sponsor, is there for help and will serve as the godfather for the couple's first baby. (Author's collection.)

The first traditional folk dance at a Greek wedding is typically the *kalamatiano*, the most basic of the folk dances that every Greek is practically required to know. The kalamatiano originated in Kalamata, Greece. Kalamata is one of the largest cities of the Pelopponese, and today caters to crowds looking for a beach, city, or village vacation. (Author's collection.)

It is never uncommon for a husband to look to his father-in-law for advice, especially in Greek culture. This man holds his young child in his arms, spending the day with his father-in-law in the early 1950s. (Courtesy of Frank Ginis.)

This photograph, taken in June 1961, proves that it was not uncommon for Greek Americans to pose at various sites around their homes and send family members the photographs. Judging from this scene, the young Ms. Themelis stands on the spot of the present-day Socrates Sculpture Park, which was transformed from an illegal dump in 1986. (Courtesy of Irene Tzivelekis.)

A festive occasion takes place at Crystal Palace catering hall in Astoria with Greek and Greek American families. Engaging in one of Greece's folk dances, onlookers celebrate by throwing money on the ground, as is shown here. The money symbolizes prosperity for all, and usually is collected by the band before the event is over. (Author's collection.)

Billy Loes, a Greek American baseball player, attended Bryant High School in the 1950s. Donning his Queens uniform before putting on his Brooklyn Dodgers uniform, Loes is rumored to have never revealed his actual last name for fear that a sportscaster would butcher it somehow. This is a feeling that most Greek people share. (Courtesy of Greater Astoria Historical Society.)

Billy Loes is carried to victory after an important 1950s baseball game. Born and raised in Queens, Billy Loes was the first Greek American to play in the major leagues. Loes was a member of the Brooklyn Dodgers 1955 championship team. (Courtesy of Greater Astoria Historical Society.)

Billy Loes played for the Brooklyn Dodgers, a huge feat for a young Greek man who had been raised in Astoria. Constantine E. Theodosiou of the Greater Astoria Historical Society relates a Loes anecdote: "In 1952 . . . he was involved in an infamous play that led to a bizarre comment on his part. When a ground ball was hit back at him, it caromed off his hip and into the outfield, allowing, I believe, two runs to score. When asked about it after the game, Billy responded that he lost the groundball in the sun!" (Courtesy of Greater Astoria Historical Society.)

As seen in the previous chapter, the 1939 world's fair drew interest for the Greek community by featuring the Greek Pavilion. Greeks from throughout the tri-state area came to see the fair and the pavilion. (Courtesy of Arie van Dort and Paul Van Dort.)

The 2004 Olympics in Athens are seen here being celebrated in Athens Square, Astoria. The Olympic torch relay made its way through all five boroughs of New York City, but began in Queens. Though Astoria is still a highly concentrated Greek community, the decision caused quite a stir throughout all of the boroughs. Greeks and people of all backgrounds gathered in the square to witness the historic event. (Courtesy of Greater Astoria Historical Society.)

ATHENA

A GIFT FROM THE PEOPLE OF
ATHENS, CAPITAL OF GREECE

TO THE PEOPLE OF
THE CITY OF NEW YORK

DIMITRIS L. AVRAMOPOULOS
MAYOR OF ATHENS

RUDOLPH W. GIULIANI
MAYOR OF NEW YORK
MARCH 1998

Shown here is the plaque of the Athena statue that still stands at Athens Square Park in Astoria. Athena was the mythological Greek goddess of wisdom and war, standing tall and proud, be it in the Athenian Parthenon or in Astoria's Little Greece. Many Greek cultural events still take place in the park, especially after its early 1990s restoration. (Author's collection.)

Athens Square Park, located on the corner of Thirtieth Street and Newtown Avenue, was named after the birthplace of democracy. Following a huge restoration in the early 1990s, it is the perfect place to hold outdoor performances and plays put on by the Greek community, especially the Greek American Folklore Society. (Photographed by Christina Rozeas.)

In 2010, Michael Gianaris became the first Greek American elected to the New York state senate. Here he shakes hands with a veteran at the Woodside Civic Association's September 11 candlelighting ceremony on the 10th anniversary of the attacks. (Courtesy of Senator Michael Gianaris.)

Senator Gianaris is pictured giving a speech, with a diverse crowd behind him. (Courtesy of Senator Michael Gianaris.)

Fruit markets, like this one, became popular in Queens with the rise of the Greek community. Many Greek businessmen invested in this idea as soon as they were financially able. (Author's collection.)

Hardworking members of the Greek American community often traveled between Manhattan and Queens in order to provide for their families and save enough to purchase their first home. Photographed here is Frank Ginis, who worked within a union to ensure financial security— something that was unheard of in Greece. (Courtesy of Frank Ginis.)

The center of Greek activity, Thirtieth Street and Broadway, has not changed much. Cafés now scatter the sidewalks, where demand grew for such businesses. By the late 1970s, Astoria was the Greek hangout and the go-to place for students coming from St. Demetrios's day school to get a bite to eat for lunch. (Author's collection.)

Six

BUSINESSES
AND ASSOCIATIONS

Shown here is the Greek American Folklore Society, after a Greek dance performance during a festival in Eisenhower Park. Located in Queens, GAFS is one of the most knowledgeable societies when it comes to Greek heritage. (Author's collection.)

THE ATHENIAN GUITAR AND BOUZOUKEE SCHOOL

PETER NICOLAOU

614 8TH AVE., NEW YORK, N.Y. 10018

TEL. 354-1125

THE ONLY GREEK-AMERICAN GUITAR & BOUZOUKEE SCHOOL IN NEW YORK

BECOME THE LIFE OF THE PARTY! LEARN TO PLAY THE GUITAR OR BOUZOUKEE QUICKLY WITH OUR OWN SIMPLE METHOD!

Evidence that history was important to talented Greeks, a *bouzoukee* school opens in Manhattan, and students from Queens and other boroughs gather there for lessons. Among them were many talented students who went on to build musical careers performing at Greek weddings and other events. (Author's collection.)

The president of the Lerian Association, Petros (Peter) Proios, leads a Greek dance during an event at Crystal Palace in Astoria. The Lerian Association is one of many Greek organizations whose goal is to bring community together and send aid wherever needed, especially when needed by countrymen in Greece. (Author's collection.)

Young girls gather outside their GOYA (Greek Orthodox Youth of America) meeting location, ready to practice dancing and to socialize with students of similar Greek background. GOYA was remains an integral part of the Greek Orthodox community. Its intention is to teach youth everything there is to know about being Greek, including holding events in order to build friendships within the community. (Courtesy of Stathoula Rozeas.)

Greek-owned shops sprang up throughout Queens. By the late 1970s, many Greek-owned businesses lined the streets of Astoria and had begun to scatter throughout the boroughs and as far as Long Island. This fish market, which was once on Willets Point Boulevard, is an example of the opportunities the Greek community sought and succeeded in upon their arrival in America. (Courtesy of Jason Antos.)

Members of a Queens-based Greek association, the Lerian Association, march on Fifth Avenue during the Greek Independence Day parade. The Federation of Hellenic Societies is one of the organizers of the Greek Independence Day parade, and every church, school, and association in the Greek community and beyond marches the streets on the day the home country of Greece declared its independence. (Courtesy of Irene Tzivelekis.)

As in America, so, too, in the old country, New Year's Eve was celebrated to bring in a new and prosperous year. This group of young people would continue to celebrate after midnight in the comfort of their own home. Even in the mid-1950s, dreams of what the journey to America would entail was the topic of conversation of many soon-to-be immigrants' last holidays in Greece. (Author's collection.)

112

Celebrating is in a Greek's blood, as is evident by the dancing that goes on at various events, such as weddings, baptisms, and even park picnics. (Author's collection.)

The youth of the Patmian's Association are all dressed up in traditional national Greek costumes, ready to perform Greek dances to keep their history alive. The traditional dance of Patmos is the *sousta*, a line dance whose name comes from the springlike steps involved. The sousta is actually the traditional line dance throughout the Dodecanse islands. (Author's collection.)

Organizations such as the Patmian's Association, pictured here, bring people together to talk history and politics from old-world and new-world perspectives. Adults and youth enjoy each other's company while partaking in the traditional Greek meal and performing line dances—the perfect things to do at this event, called a *xorosperida* (dinner dance). (Author's collection.)

Greeks have helped out their fellow countrymen by offering them their business, and this has kept Greek-owned establishments more than afloat. An example of Greek Americans patronizing countrymen's businesses is this bridal portrait, taken in a Greek-owned Astoria photography studio. (Author's collection.)

Titan Foods, now located on Thirty-first Street in Astoria, is the largest Greek supermarket in Queens. If one has an urge to check out authentic Greek foods straight from the old country, Titan is usually the place to turn. A couple of generations of Greek Americans have grown up with the store. (Author's collection.)

Neptune Diner has been a staple in the Greek community, and in the larger Astoria community, for the past 60 or so years. Located under the el, Neptune has been the setting for many a Saturday morning meal or a Sunday after-church brunch. (Author's collection.)

Newly arrived immigrants from Greece noticed that there were absolutely no *cafenia* (coffee shops) in Queens. Back in the old country, these were a necessity, to meet outside the home in order to discuss local and world news, religion, and politics. Thankfully, Greek Americans, like those in this photograph, began to incorporate this lifestyle into the Queens community. This is now evident if you drive down Astoria's Thirtieth Avenue. (Author's collection.)

The Archbishop requested that the "Philoptochos plan many events for the entire family, featuring music, lectures, performances, sponsoring bazaars and the St. Basil's pita, charging a small admission fee and having a raffle. For the children, develop a separate club under your Chapter, which should have its own President, present children's observances and meetings, so that the youth will become accustomed to your good example and will be of greater interest to them". He asked that they study the By-laws and implement them for edification of Greek Orthodox Christians in America.

"Please contact the City Hall, the Welfare Department and the American philanthropic offices in your city to make your work more fruitful.

"The Archdiocese has acquired two homes and orphanages at Pomfret, Connecticut, and the St. Stefanos' Monastery at Gastonia, North Carolina. It is urgent that we establish a children's home and orphanage and I would be happy if you would undertake the sustenance of the orphans of the community."

This historic encyclical inaugurated the National Philoptochos Society, encompassing every aspect of service Archbishop Athenagoras envisioned for the organization to assist the Greek Orthodox community.

Following this initial encyclical from Archbishop Athenagoras granting official status to the Ladies Philoptochos as an Archdiocesan philanthropic organization, the mission of the Adelphotis began in earnest to comply with the By-laws and to serve effectively the Greek community.

In October, 1935, the first general assembly of the Philoptochos Adelphotis was convened in Boston with Archbishop Athenagoras presiding. The sessions were held in the Saints Constantine and Helen Church in Cambridge, Mass. In his letter to the Philoptochos Chapters and the other women's clubs invited to participate, the Archbishop listed the following:

The Hotel Minerva in Boston was designated to house the delegates. Room rates $2.00 per day.

Luncheon was available at a cost of .50 cents. Dinner at a cost of .75 cents.

A letter from His Holiness Patriarch Photios was read to the delegates and elicited great joy among the ladies.

Archbishop Athenagoras addressed many communications to the women, over the years, offering suggestions, counseling their efforts, praising their accomplishments, as he did on June 17, 1936, stating in an encyclical to the Priests, Board of Trustees and all Greek Orthodox Christians in the Archdiocese: "the mission promoted by the Philoptochos in many parishes has accomplished miracles". On another occasion the Archbishop offered many suggestions to increase the membership of the Philoptochos in order to aid the poor. He asked that the ladies be concerned for the school and the students who are poor; he asked that the Feastday of Saints Cosmas and Damianos, which is observed on November 1st, he

Delegation to the 1st Convention, Boston, Mass., October 7, 1935.

24

The origins of the Philoptochos Society can be found in October 1935, when the first general assembly of the Philoptochos Adelphotis convened in Boston, with Archbishop Athenagoras presiding. This gave birth to a society in which women were able to offer their philanthropic services and contribute to the community where help was needed. It was the type of association that brings church and community together, facilitated by various events and communications. (Courtesy of Vivian Siempos and the Greek Orthodox Ladies Philoptochos Society.)

Philoptochos Society "Annunciation"
Assumption Greek Orthodox Cathedral
4610 E. Alameda Avenue, Denver, CO 80222

ORGANIZED 1947/CHARTERED 1948
Rev. Meletios Deacandrew, *Founding Priest*

FIRST BOARD OF DIRECTORS
Mary Gates, *President*
Helen Tamaresis, *Vice-President*
Alexandra Pann, *1st Secretary*
Ourania Angelo, *2nd Secretary*
Dena Papageorge, *Treasurer*

CHARTER MEMBERS
Mary Demos
Georgia Rador
Hrisoula Hatzotolou
Helen Arapkilies
Katrine Mauries
Irene Kavas
Demitra Diamantopoulou
Marie Khochiovelos
Athanacia Allison
Zaharoula Ferres
Anastacia Arapkilies
Stavroula Vassilopoulou
Stamatia Maniatis
Anna Tasinas
Mary Gates
Helen Tamaresis
Dena Papageorge
Alexandra Pann
Ourania Angelo

PAST PRESIDENTS
Mary Gates
Alexandra Pann
Virginia Pappas
Dena Papageorge
Estelle Rador
Christine Pavlakis
Florence Garyet
Tula Maniatis
Connie Maniatis

1st row (left to right): Fotoula Skaliotes, Zaharoula Ferris, Dena N. Papageorge, 1st Treasurer, Mary A. Gates, 1st President of Philoptochos, Archbishop Athenagoras, Rev. Meletios Deacandrew, Alexandra Pann, 1st Secretary. 2nd row: Libby Fotinos, Ourania Angelitch, Irene Kavas, Aspasia Maniatis, Mary Demos, Helen Tamaresis, 1st Vice-President, Tula Diamond. 3rd row: Maria Kechiovelos, Esther Pantels, Helen T. Dikeou, Helen Arapkilies, Stamatia Maniatis.

186

The Heights Diner, shown here, was once located on Northern Boulevard in Jackson Heights. A group of Greek men purchased the diner as partners in 1954. Diners quickly became known as being distinctly Greek, as most diners located in Queens were, at one point, Greek owned. (Courtesy of Maria Caputo.)

SKOURAS THEATRES
For Better Entertainment

BAYSIDE	ROOSEVELT
BELL BOULEVARD BAyside 9 - 9608	**160th ST. & NORTHERN BLV** FLushing 9 - 9600

BAYSIDE	ROOSEVELT
Thurs.-Sat. Jan. 27-29 "LILI" "PARIS PLAYBOYS"	Thurs.-Sat. Jan. 27 "WHITE CHRISTMA "VISTA VISION VISITS NORW
Sun.-Tues. Jan.-Feb. 1 in cinemascope "DRUMBEAT" "PASSION"	Sun.-Tues. Jan. 30-Fe "CARMEN JONES "THE OUTLAW's daughter"
Starts Wed. Feb. 2 "CARMEN JONES"	Wed. Feb. "LILI" "FIRE OVER AFRIC
Sat. SPECIAL KIDDIE SHOW 3rd. Big Feature	Sat. Jan CHILDRENS SHOW 11 a.m "MONTANA TERRITORY"

The Skouras Theaters were named after the Skouras brothers, who arrived from Greece around 1910. This advertisement ran in the *Bayside Times* for much of 1955. Movie theaters throughout Queens were often crowded on the weekends and holidays with Greek cinema-lovers. (Courtesy of the Bayside Historical Society.)

By the 1920s, Greeks began owning and operating their own businesses. In Far Rockaway, on Corneda Avenue, the owners of a hat- and shoe-cleaning parlor stand in their doorway. Spiros Papouchis (right) had accomplished a feat he would not have been able to had he remained in Greece. The phrase "Land of Opportunity" rang true, and continues to do so, for such immigrants. (Courtesy of Constantine E. Theodosiou.)

Stamatis is king of the Greek restaurants in Astoria, and in the past decade has become even more popular among non-Greek clientele for its incredible cuisine. Among the home-cooked recipes offered are *gemista* (stuffed tomatoes), and *xoriatiki salata* (which translates roughly to "salad from the village"). (Author's collection.)

Mediterranean supermarkets have spread throughout Queens over the years, and picking up your groceries always tempted the buyer to sample a Kalamata olive or a piece of feta cheese. (Author's collection.)

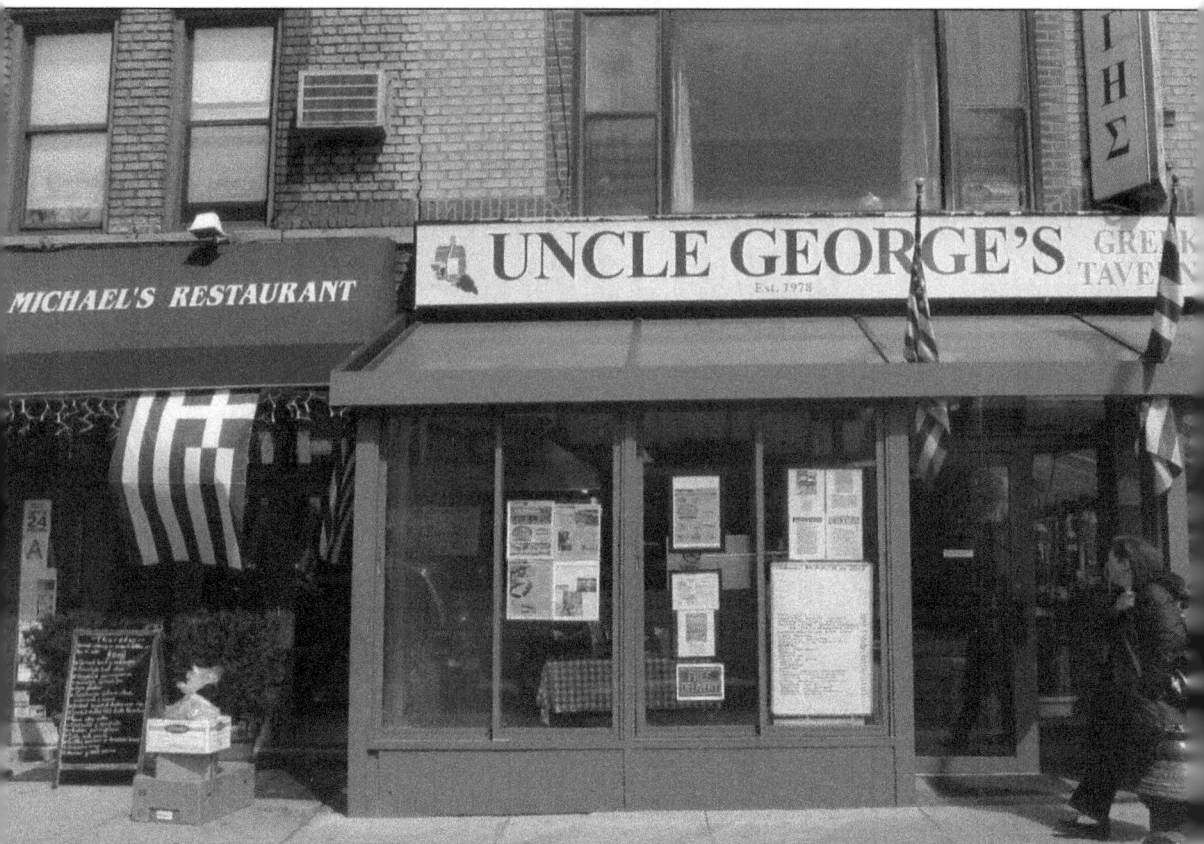

The Greek tavern Uncle George's has been around longer than many places in Astoria; thus, this "Greek corner" on a busy street is still thriving at all hours of the night. (Author's collection.)

Omonia, one of Queens's oldest *cafenia* (coffee shops), is owned by John Arvanitis. In the 1970s, he noticed Queens was missing coffee shops, which in Greece are an integral part of socializing. (Author's collection.)

Oasis Café picks up where Omonia and various Astoria coffeehouses leave off. Located on Northern Boulevard in Flushing, Oasis is central to members of the Greek American community. Flushing residents of all ages are familiar with Oasis. (Author's collection.)

ΚΕΝΤΡΟ ΕΛΛΗΝΙΚΟΥ ΠΟΛΙΤΙΣΜΟΥ
GREEK CULTURAL CENTER

ΣΥΝΑΥΛΙΑ ΑΦΙΕΡΩΜΑ ΣΤΟΝ ΟΔΥΣΣΕΑ ΕΛΥΤΗ
τον ποιητή που τιμήθηκε με το βραβείο Νόμπελ της λογοτεχνίας το 1979

CONCERT TRIBUTE TO ODYSSEUS ELYTIS
The Nobel Prize winner in literature 1979

SATURDAY FEBRUARY 25, 2012 7.00

Frank Sinatra School of the Arts
35-12 35th Avenue Astoria, NY 11106

For tickets and information
call :718-726-7329

Music by **VASILIS LEKKAS** and his band Stathis Savvidis,Apostolos Tsardakas, Ioannis Filipoupolitis, who are coming from Greece to perform at this Concert for one and only performance. Special excerpts from "Axion Esti" set to music by Mikis Theodorakis will be performed as well as songs by other Greek composers like M. Hatzidakis, M.Loizos, S.Xarhakos, J. Markopoulos, L. Kokotos , N. Mavroudis and others who were inspired by the great Poet.

26-80 30th Street Astoria, NY 11102
Tel: 718-726–7629 Fax: 718-210-3359
e-mail: info@greekculturalcenter.org

ΟΔΥΣΣΕΑΣ ΕΛΥΤΗΣ

The Greek Cultural Center is a nonprofit organization that has been around since the early 1970s. This image proves that Greeks still love to perform historical and modern plays by influential playwrights. The cultural center caters to the community by teaching the arts and Greek culture to all who are willing to learn. (Courtesy of the Greek Cultural Center.)

Visit us at
arcadiapublishing.com

www.ingramcontent.com/pod-product-compliance
Lightning Source LLC
Chambersburg PA
CBHW050628110426
42813CB00007B/1746

* 9 7 8 1 5 3 1 6 6 5 8 4 5 *